W9-AVL-978

Gemstones

ANN O. SQUIRE

Children's Press®
An Imprint of Scholastic Inc.
New York   Toronto   London   Auckland   Sydney
Mexico City   New Delhi   Hong Kong
Danbury, Connecticut

Content Consultant
Vicki Harder
Associate Professor
Department of Natural Sciences
Western New Mexico University
Silver City, NM

Library of Congress Cataloging-in-Publication Data

Squire, Ann.
  Gemstones/by Ann O. Squire.
     pages cm—(A true book)
  Includes bibliographical references and index.
  ISBN-13: 978-0-531-26143-9 (lib. bdg.) — ISBN-13: 978-0-531-26251-1 (pbk.)
1. Precious stones—Juvenile literature. I. Title.
  QE392.2.S69 2012
  553.8—dc23

All rights reserved. Published in 2013 by Children's Press, an imprint of Scholastic Inc.
Printed in China 62
SCHOLASTIC, CHILDREN'S PRESS, A TRUE BOOK™, and associated logos are trademarks and/or registered trademarks of Scholastic Inc.
1 2 3 4 5 6 7 8 9 10 R 22 21 20 19 18 17 16 15 14 13

Front cover: cut diamonds
Back cover: natural crystals

Find the Truth!

Everything you are about to read is true *except* for one of the sentences on this page.

Which one is **TRUE**?

T or F Diamonds are the rarest of all gemstones.

T or F Sapphires can be blue, yellow, green, purple, pink, or colorless.

Find the answers in this book.

Contents

THE **BIG** TRUTH!

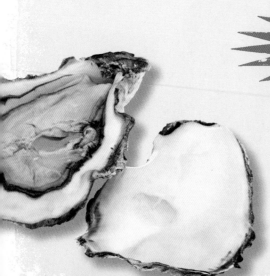

4

An insect encased in amber

People have worn gems as birthstones for hundreds of years.

5

Britain's crown jewels have been kept at the Tower of London since the 1300s.

CHAPTER 1

Dazzling Diamonds and Elegant Emeralds

Throughout history, gemstones have been associated with wealth and power. Royal families in many countries have owned sets of crown jewels. These jewels symbolized a family's right to rule over their nation's people. Kings, queens, and emperors had crowns and scepters, or staffs, studded with gems. Some of these pieces were very elaborate.

Crystals

Most gemstones are **minerals**. A mineral is a natural substance, which means that humans did not create it. A mineral is solid and always has a **crystal**-like structure. This gives it straight edges, flat faces, and a geometric shape, such as a pyramid or a cube. Crystals form deep underground and can take millions of years to grow. After being mined, rough gemstones must be cut and polished to reveal their true beauty.

An uncut gemstone is called a raw gemstone.

Gemstones such as ammolite (above) are often found within rocks.

Is It a Gemstone?

How can a person tell if a crystal is a gemstone or a just a common mineral? A crystal must pass three tests to be called a gemstone. First, it must be beautiful. It also needs to be hard. Lastly, it must be rare. A mineral might live up to one or two of these factors, but would still not be considered a valuable gemstone.

A gemstone is usually cut from a single, large crystal.

A Beautiful Stone

Different gemstones can be considered beautiful for different reasons. For example, a diamond is considered beautiful because of its ability to **refract** light. When you look at a diamond in the sunlight, you can see all the colors of the rainbow. Rubies, sapphires, and emeralds are prized for their clear, rich colors.

Made to Last

Gemstone crystals should be very difficult to scratch. In 1812, a **mineralogist** named Friedrich Mohs developed a scale to rank the hardness of minerals. The diamond is at the top of the list. Not only is it the hardest gemstone, it is also the hardest substance known to humans! Rubies and sapphires are the next-hardest gemstones. Topaz, quartz, and emeralds are farther down on Mohs' scale.

Friedrich Mohs' scale is still used to analyze rocks and minerals today.

Rare Crystals

The third requirement for a gemstone is rarity. A crystal must be quite large for someone to be able to cut a gem from it. For a crystal to grow to a large size, conditions must be just right. The growing crystal needs the proper temperature, enough time, enough space, and the right materials. Because of this, crystals that are large enough to become gems are very rare in the natural world.

A miner pans for gems, separating rare gemstones from mud and rocks.

Weighing Gemstones

Gemologists use a special unit of measurement to describe the weight of gemstones: a **carat**. *Carat* comes from the word *carob*, a kind of seed. In ancient times, gem dealers weighed their stones by comparing them to the weight of a carob seed. A gem that equaled the weight of one seed would be a 1-carob (1-carat) stone. This equals about 0.007 ounces (0.2 grams). There are 5 carats in a gram and 2,268 carats in a pound.

CHAPTER 2

Out of the Earth

Different gemstones are formed in different ways. But they all start deep below the surface of the earth. Earth's outer layer, called the crust, is made up of solid rock. Below the crust is a layer called the mantle. Temperatures in the mantle are high enough to melt rock. Pressure is also very high, which keeps the melted rock from moving. When the pressure is released, the rock rises and becomes **molten** rock, called **magma**.

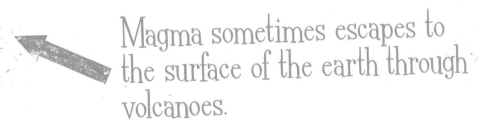

Magma sometimes escapes to the surface of the earth through volcanoes.

Created by Heat

Many miles below earth's surface, superheated magma is constantly pushing upward against the crust. If the pressure becomes too great, the crust can crack. Some magma escapes, flowing upward through the crust. If the magma breaks through to the earth's surface, it comes out as lava from an erupting volcano. If it does not break through, the magma hardens between layers of rock in the crust.

This diagram shows magma (in orange) as it moves up through a volcano or is trapped under the surface.

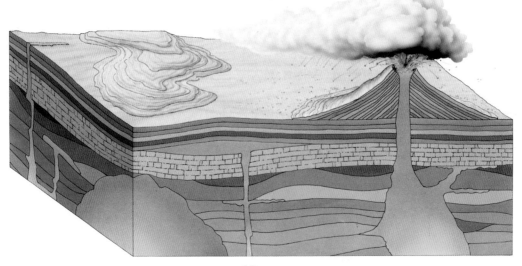

This emerald crystal grew as the material around it hardened into rock.

Within the magma are tiny mineral crystals.
As the magma slowly cools, these crystals grow.
If the conditions are right and the magma has
the correct ingredients, the crystals can form
gemstones. Gems that are formed in this way are
called **igneous**, which means "made by heat."
Igneous gemstones include emeralds, quartzes,
garnets, and topazes.

Opal is often found in seams between layers of sedimentary rock.

Under Pressure

Some gemstones are created through pressure. Wind and water slowly weather, or break down, rocks in the earth's crust. The rocks are broken into smaller pieces called sediment. Over time, layers of sediment build up, putting pressure on lower layers. This pressure, along with high temperatures, causes such gemstones as diamonds to form.

On the Surface

If most gemstones are formed miles below the earth's surface, how did people ever discover them? Weathering is the answer. Because gemstones are very hard, weathering does not affect them much. But centuries of wind and rain do wear away the layers of rock surrounding the gemstones. This erosion leaves the precious crystals closer to the earth's surface, where they can be mined.

Weathering brings gemstones closer to the surface, but miners often still have to dig thousands of feet into the ground to find them.

Amber is prized for its transparency, allowing light to pass through it.

CHAPTER 3

Animal, Vegetable, or Mineral?

Most gems are minerals, made up of materials that were not part of a living organism. But there are a few gemstones that come from **organic** sources. Pearls, coral, and amber are some examples. All three are often used in jewelry. Because they can pass the test of beauty, durability, and rarity, these materials are considered to be gems.

Pearls

Oysters, clams, and mussels are responsible for the world's most famous organic gem, the pearl. Most pearls come from oysters. To understand how pearls are formed, it helps to know the parts of an oyster. Oysters, like clams and mussels, have a two-part shell. Inside the shell is the mantle, an organ that produces a substance called nacre. Nacre is a smooth material that forms the lining of the shell.

Nacre is also called mother-of-pearl.

Once a pearl is large enough, it can be removed from the oyster and used as a gemstone.

An Irritating Situation

Oysters normally rest with their shells partway open, taking in water to obtain oxygen and food. Sometimes a grain of sand or other debris is sucked in along with the water. The debris can then slip between the mantle and the shell. This irritates the oyster's soft body. In response, the mantle produces nacre and covers the sharp object with layer upon layer of smooth material. Over several years, a pearl is formed.

Natural pearls are almost never perfectly round.

Baroque Pearls

The most valuable pearls, and the ones most often used in jewelry, are perfectly round. But pearls don't always form completely round. Sometimes pearls come out lumpy, bumpy, oval, or teardrop-shaped. These are called baroque pearls. And did you know that not all pearls are white? They can be pink, gray, black, or almost any other color you can think of. The color of a pearl depends on the type of oyster that produced it.

Cultured Pearls

Natural pearls are very rare. As a result, people developed ways of producing pearls artificially. It is possible to force an oyster to make a pearl by putting a tiny bead inside the oyster's shell. The resulting pearl is called a cultured pearl. It looks so much like a natural pearl that it must be x-rayed to show the difference. But because cultured pearls are not as rare as natural pearls, they are usually less valuable.

Pearl farms in Polynesia are known for producing black pearls.

Coral

Coral is another gem that comes from the sea. Coral polyps are tiny marine animals that live in colonies. As the polyps grow, a hard skeleton forms around them. It is this reddish-pink skeleton that is used in jewelry. The ancient Romans believed that coral had magical powers. They wore pieces of coral to protect them from harm. They also thought that coral could be used to cure snake and scorpion bites.

Living coral comes in countless colors, including neon green.

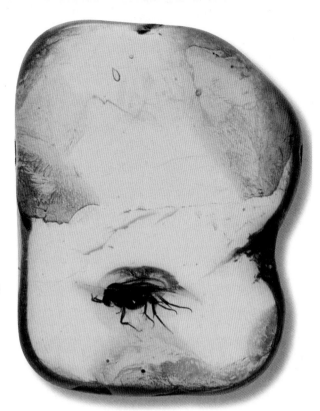

Amber is most valuable if it includes an insect or other ancient remains.

Amber

Amber is another organic gem that comes from an unlikely source. Amber is the **fossilized** sap from ancient pine trees. The oldest amber ever found dates from the Upper Carboniferous period, which took place 320 million years ago. Amber sometimes contains the remains of insects that were trapped in the sticky tree sap. Amber is soft in comparison to other gems, and is often used in beads and necklaces.

The Real Thing?

What if gemstones could be created in a laboratory? This was the dream of scientists for hundreds of years. In 1837, a French chemist came up with a method to make rubies in his laboratory. However, his first stones were not clear or beautiful enough to use in jewelry.

Over the years, technology improved. Now, rubies, diamonds, sapphires, emeralds, and other gems are created in laboratories. These are exact copies of natural gemstones. A natural diamond, mined from the earth, is made of the same mineral and has the same structure as one that comes from a laboratory. The difference is that the natural one takes millions of years to grow and the man-made one takes only three days!

Uncut laboratory-made sapphires (left) and ruby (right)

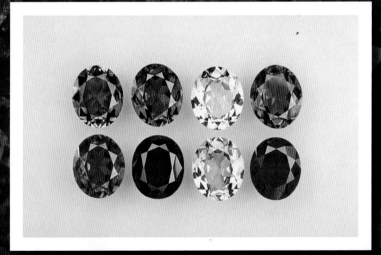

Cut laboratory-made sapphires and rubies

30

CHAPTER 4

A Rainbow of Colors

Rubies, emeralds, sapphires, and aquamarines are all known for their rich colors. But did you know that the minerals these gemstones are made of could be completely colorless? And when you think of a diamond, you might imagine a clear, colorless gem. But this is not always true. Diamonds can be yellow, blue, green, pink, violet, brown, or even black!

The Hope diamond is named after the family who owned it in the 1800s.

Sapphires can be
heated to enhance
their natural colors.

Rubies and Sapphires

Rubies and sapphires are made of the same
mineral, corundum. Pure corundum can be
colorless. Small traces of certain minerals give
corundum a variety of colors, creating completely
different-looking gemstones. Corundum with
a trace of chromium has the deep, red color of
a ruby. Iron and titanium turn corundum into a
sapphire. Sapphires can be blue, pink, yellow,
green, purple, or colorless.

Lucky Stars

Corundum crystals sometimes include tiny needlelike fibers of a mineral called rutile. When light reflects off these fibers, it gives the appearance of a six-pointed star. The star seems to move when viewed from different

The Rosser Reeves Star Ruby is kept at the Smithsonian Institute in Washington, D.C.

angles. A corundum gem that includes rutile is called a star sapphire or star ruby. These gems are usually cut with a rounded and polished top. One of the world's largest star sapphires, the Star of India, weighs 563 carats.

Beryl is colored red by the mineral manganese.

The Beryl Family

Beryl is another colorless mineral that can look very different with various trace minerals. Green emeralds, blue aquamarines, yellow heliodor, and pink morganite are all varieties of beryl. Red beryl, also known as red emerald, is only mined in the Wah Wah Mountains of Utah. Red beryl is much rarer than diamonds. For every 150,000 diamonds that are mined, just one red beryl crystal is found.

What's Your Birthstone?

Ancient cultures believed that a gemstone's magic was strongest in the month to which it "belonged." Use the list to the right to find the stone belonging to the month in which you were born. Some months have more than one birthstone, so you can choose the one you like best.

January	Garnet
February	Amethyst
March	Aquamarine
April	Diamond
May	Emerald
June	Pearl or Alexandrite
July	Ruby
August	Peridot
September	Sapphire
October	Tourmaline or Opal
November	Topaz or Citrine
December	Tanzanite, Zircon, or Turquoise

Dazzling Diamonds

Diamonds are made of the element carbon. Unlike many other gemstones, diamonds are usually valued for their lack of color. Still, traces of minerals found in carbon can give diamonds some unique colors. One well-known colored diamond is the Hope Diamond, which weighs more than 45 carats. With its beautiful deep blue color, it is easy to mistake this diamond for a sapphire. The 41-carat Dresden Diamond is green and looks very much like an emerald.

A Timeline of Diamonds

3.3 billion–990 million years ago
Today's diamonds form in cooling magma.

320–296 BCE
Diamonds are first described in India.

Cutting a Diamond

It takes a skillful diamond cutter to shape an uncut diamond to reveal its brilliance. But how does someone cut the world's hardest substance? Diamonds are weak along the natural faces of their crystals. This makes it possible to break a diamond into smaller pieces. When cutters shape diamonds by hand, they use other diamonds. A diamond can also be sawed. A phosphor-bronze blade can cut a diamond, spinning at 15,000 rounds per minute.

1458 CE
Lodewyk van Berquem of Belgium creates the first cut diamond.

1477
The first recorded diamond engagement ring is given by Archduke Maximilian of Austria to Mary of Burgundy.

1866
A child discovers the first diamond in Africa, mistaking it for a pebble.

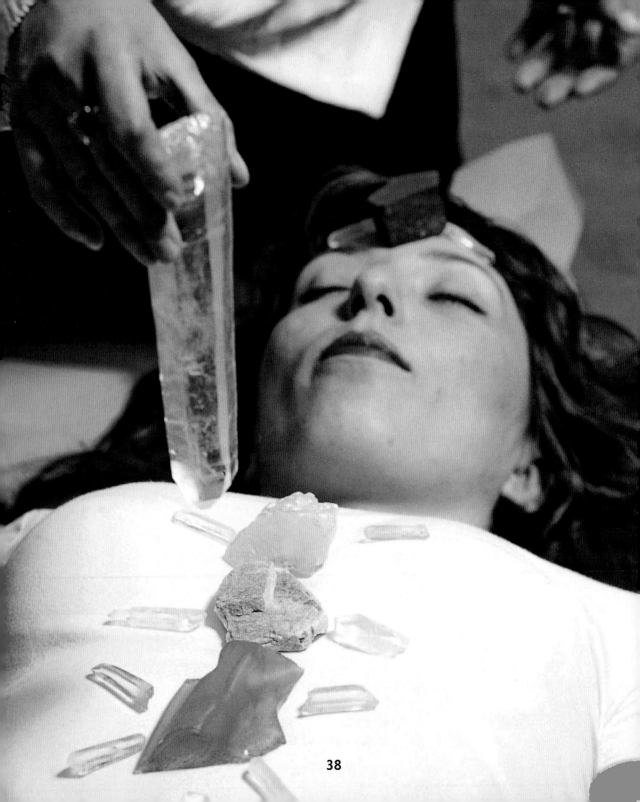

CHAPTER 5

Useful Gems

Under the right conditions, minerals can shine as gemstones. They can grace jewelry, be used as money, or sit on display in museums for millions of visitors to see. But even when not on display, these minerals can be valuable. They often play important parts in our everyday lives, making blades sharper, metals stronger, and instruments more accurate and longer lasting.

Some people believe gems such as amethyst can help improve a person's health.

Industrial Diamonds

As the hardest mineral on Earth, diamonds can be used to cut any material. Small diamond pieces can be used to cut glass. Diamonds can also be crushed into a fine powder, which can grind or polish diamonds and other gemstones for jewelry. The powder is also used in saw and drill blades, making them stronger and sharper. These diamond-studded tools are used to cut through rock, tile, and other hard materials.

Saws made with diamonds can cut granite and other building materials.

40

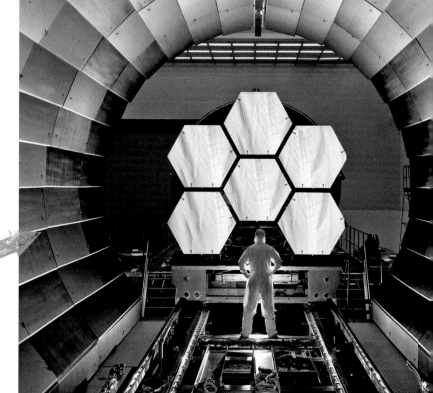

NASA's James Webb Space Telescope has beryllium in its mirrors.

Space Age Mineral

Emeralds can be a valuable beryl gemstone. Even as a plain mineral, beryl is valuable. It is a major source of beryllium, a metal similar to aluminum. Beryllium is one-third stronger than steel. It is often mixed with copper to add strength. It is also very lightweight and is used in space vehicles and high-speed aircraft.

Sapphires are used in watch crystals, the clear coverings that protect the watch face.

A Tough Mineral

Whether sparkling as a sapphire or as a common mineral, corundum has distinctive features. Its barrel-shaped crystals make it easy to recognize. It is also 9 on Mohs' hardness scale, just under diamonds. For this reason, it is often used to make **abrasive** materials, such as sandpaper. Sapphires are also used in watches and scientific instruments because of their durability.

Modern Fascination

Throughout history, gemstones have been prized for their beauty and rarity. Today, these minerals and gemstones are everywhere, from rings on fingers to drills in mines. Mining, cutting, and laboratory technology has improved over the centuries, making these stones more available. As more people can afford them and more uses are found, gemstones retain their hold on our imaginations. ★

Gemstones are used to create elaborate jewelry.

43

True Statistics

World's largest diamond-producing country: Russia, producing nearly 35 million carats in 2010.

Amount of ore that must be mined to produce 1 carat of diamonds: 10 tons or more

Weight of the world's largest natural pearl: 14.1 lb. (6.4 kg)

Weight of the world's largest emerald: 858 carats

Number of faces on the world's largest diamond: 74

Number of years it takes for a cultured pearl to form: 2 to 3

Number of years it takes for a natural diamond to form: 1 billion to 3 billion

Distance beneath the earth's surface at which diamonds form: More than 75 mi. (121 km)

Did you find the truth?

F Diamonds are the rarest of all gemstones.

T Sapphires can be blue, yellow, green, purple, pink, or colorless.

Resources

Books

Bonewitz, Ronald Louis. *Rock and Gem*. New York: DK Publishing, 2008.

Finlay, Victoria. *Jewels: A Secret History*. New York: Ballantine Books, 2006.

Polk, Patti. *Collecting Rocks, Gems and Minerals: Identification, Values, Lapidary Uses*. Iola, WI: Krause Publications, Inc., 2010.

Symes, R. F., and R. R. Harding. *Crystal & Gem*. New York: DK Publishing, 2007.

Trueit, Trudi Strain. *Rocks, Gems, and Minerals*. New York: Franklin Watts, 2003.

Visit this Scholastic Web site for more information on gemstones:
★ www.factsfornow.scholastic.com
Enter the keyword **Gemstones**

Important Words

abrasive (uh-BRAY-siv) — rough and coarse

carat (KAR-uht) — a unit for measuring the weight of gemstones

crystal (KRIS-tuhl) — a substance that forms a pattern of many flat surfaces when it becomes a solid

fossilized (FAH-suh-lyzed) — hardened and preserved over time

gemologists (jem-AH-luh-jists) — people who study gems

igneous (IG-nee-uhs) — produced by great heat

magma (MAG-muh) — melted rock found beneath the earth's surface that is called lava when it flows out of volcanoes

mineralogist (min-ur-AH-luh-jist) — a person who studies minerals

minerals (MIN-ur-uhlz) — solid substances found in the earth that do not come from an animal or plant

molten (MOHL-tuhn) — melted at a high temperature

organic (or-GAN-ik) — from or produced by living things

refract (ri-FRAKT) — bend, as when a ray of light enters another medium, such as water or glass

Index

Page numbers in **bold** indicate illustrations

About the Author

Ann O. Squire is a psychologist and an animal behaviorist. Before becoming a writer, she studied the behavior of rats, tropical fish in the Caribbean, and electric fish from Central Africa. Her favorite part of being a writer is the chance to learn as much as she can about all sorts of topics. In addition to *Gemstones*, *Fossils*, *Rocks*, and *Minerals*, Dr. Squire has written about many different animals, from lemmings to leopards and cicadas to cheetahs. She lives in Katonah, New York.